ISLES OF SCILLY TRAVEL GUIDE 2024

"The complete insider guide to exploring the best of Isles of Scilly Cornwall, England beaches, outdoor activities, culture, adventure, hiking, festivals and events, hidden gems"

Mercy Davis

TABLE OF CONTENTS

Introduction

Nestled off the southwestern tip of Cornwall, the Isles of Scilly emerge like a scattering of precious gems adrift in the Atlantic Ocean. A destination that seems painted by the whims of nature's gentlest brushstrokes, the Isles of Scilly beckon with an enchanting allure that captivates the soul and sparks the imagination.

As you embark on this journey to the Isles, envision a world where time slows and the everyday hustle yields to the rhythm of the tides. Each archipelago's islands, whether the bustling St. Mary's or the serene Tresco, contribute to a narrative that unfolds against a backdrop of crystalline waters, golden sands, and blooming heathlands.

It is a land where history whispers through the ancient stone walls of Cromwell's Castle and where the call of seabirds carries the echoes of seafaring tales that resonate through the ages. But the Isles of Scilly are not mere relics of the past; they are a living canvas where the past seamlessly intertwines with the present, creating a tapestry of cultural richness.

Unspoiled by the clamor of modernity, the Isles offer a sanctuary for those seeking respite from the cacophony of urban life. Immerse yourself in the vibrant hues of subtropical gardens, where exotic flora flourishes in a climate that defies the typical British weather. Whether wandering through the Abbey Gardens on Tresco or exploring the windswept moors of Bryher, nature here is a masterful artist, weaving a palette of colors that dance in harmony with the changing seasons.

In this travel guide, we invite you to uncover the secrets of the Isles of Scilly – to meander along footpaths that reveal breathtaking vistas, to savor the flavors of locally sourced cuisine, and to connect with a community that thrives in harmony with its surroundings. Each island has a distinct personality, and together, they create a destination where the world's relentless pace yields a more serene and contemplative rhythm.

Prepare to be enchanted by the Isles of Scilly, where time seems to stand still, and every moment becomes a chapter in a story written by the sea, the wind, and the resilient spirit of its people. Welcome to a destination that transcends the ordinary – where tranquility is not just a state of being but a way of life.

Why Visit the Isles of Scilly?

1. **Unspoiled Natural Beauty:** Immerse yourself in a world where nature takes center stage. From pristine beaches with crystal-clear waters to vibrant subtropical gardens and rugged coastal cliffs, the Isles of Scilly boast unspoiled landscapes that inspire awe at every turn.

2. **Tranquil Escape:** Escape the hustle and bustle of modern life as you step into a realm where time seems to slow down. The laid-back atmosphere and absence of crowded tourist hotspots create an ideal environment for relaxation and rejuvenation.

3. **Unique Island Character:** Each inhabited island, from the largest, St. Mary's, to the smallest, St. Agnes, has its distinct character and charm. Explore the diversity of landscapes, traditions, and local communities, creating a tapestry of enriching and diverse experiences.

4. **Historical Riches:** Delve into the rich history of the Isles, where ancient stone structures and remnants of a maritime past

tell stories of bygone eras. Visit castles, churches, and archaeological sites that witness centuries of human presence and resilience against the elements.

5. **Outdoor Adventures:** Whether you're an avid hiker, water sports enthusiast, or nature lover, the Isles of Scilly cater to various outdoor activities. Traverse scenic walking trails, embark on boat excursions, or dive into the azure waters for a snorkeling or kayaking adventure.

6. **Unique Flora and Fauna:** Witness a unique blend of subtropical and maritime climates that give rise to a diverse array of flora and fauna. Rare plants, vibrant wildflowers, and prolific birdlife make the Isles of Scilly a haven for nature enthusiasts and birdwatchers.

7. **Local Cuisine and Culture:** Indulge in the local flavors of Scillonian cuisine, characterized by fresh seafood, locally sourced produce, and traditional recipes. Immerse yourself in the welcoming local culture, where a strong sense of community and a slower pace of life prevail.

8. **Serene Beaches:** Discover secluded coves and pristine beaches, inviting you to unwind against azure waters. Whether you seek solitude or a family-friendly setting, the Isles offer a variety of beaches, each with its unique charm.

9. **Ethical and Sustainable Tourism:** Embrace a travel destination committed to sustainability and responsible tourism. The Isles of Scilly take pride in preserving their natural environment and heritage, offering visitors a chance to experience a destination where conservation is a shared responsibility.

10. **Magical Atmosphere:** There's an undeniable magic in the air of the Isles of Scilly, a feeling that transcends the tangible and leaves visitors with a sense of connection to the land and sea. It's an atmosphere that lingers, inviting you to return and explore more of the enchanting archipelago.

In essence, the Isles of Scilly promise not just a vacation but an immersive journey into a world where time moves at its own pace and the beauty of the natural environment is a constant companion. Whether seeking adventure, relaxation, or a glimpse into a unique culture, the Isles of Scilly beckon as a destination where dreams and reality seamlessly converge.

Getting Started

Embarking on a journey to the Isles of Scilly is like stepping into a realm where time moves unhurriedly, and nature unfolds in all its pristine glory. To ensure that your vacation is as seamless as the archipelago's turquoise waters, let's delve into the essential details of getting started, from planning your trip to navigating the transportation options.

Planning Your Trip: Crafting Your Scilly Escape

Before setting foot on this enchanting archipelago, meticulous planning ensures every moment is spent in blissful exploration. Here are key considerations to guide your journey:

- **Researching the Isles:** Begin your journey by delving into the unique characteristics of each island. St. Mary's, the largest, is a hub of activity, while the smaller islands like St. Agnes offer serene retreats. Understand the diverse landscapes, cultural offerings, and activities each island presents.

- **Accommodation Choices:** The Isles of Scilly offer a range of accommodation options, from charming bed and breakfasts to luxury hotels. Consider your preferences and budget when selecting a place to stay, and book well in advance, especially during peak seasons.

- **Activity Planning:** Tailor your itinerary based on your interests. Whether you're drawn to historical sites, outdoor adventures, or simply unwinding on pristine beaches, the Isles cater to various preferences. Plan activities on different islands to make the most of your visit.

Best Time to Visit: Unveiling Scilly's Seasonal Charms

The Isles of Scilly cast a spell that's equally mesmerizing in every season, but understanding the nuances of each can elevate your experience:

- **Spring (March to May):** Witness the islands bloom as spring unfolds. Wildflowers carpet the landscape, and migratory birds make their return. The mild weather makes it an ideal time for hiking and birdwatching.

- **Summer (June to August):** The Isles truly come alive in summer. Enjoy long daylight hours, warm temperatures, and a calendar filled with events and festivals. Dive into the crystalline waters, explore coastal trails, and savor the vibrant ambiance.

- **Autumn (September to November):** As summer bids farewell, autumn unveils a quieter charm. The islands transition into hues of gold and copper. It's an excellent time for peaceful walks, cultural events, and enjoying the last traces of warmth before winter sets in.

- **Winter (December to February):** Winter offers a different perspective, with a uniquely Scillonian tranquility. While some facilities may close for the season, the islands' beauty remains, and you might find yourself practically alone on the stunning beaches.

Duration of Stay: Crafting Your Scilly Sojourn

The ideal duration for a visit to the Isles of Scilly depends on your preferences and the activities you plan to engage in. Here are general recommendations:

- **Short Getaway (3-4 Days):** Perfect for a weekend escape or a short break, focusing on one or two islands. It is ideal for those seeking a quick retreat and a taste of Scilly's beauty.

- **Extended Stay (7-10 Days):** For a more immersive experience, you can explore multiple islands and engage in various activities. This duration is ideal for a comprehensive discovery of the archipelago.

- **Seasonal Exploration (2 Weeks or More):** Consider a longer stay if you wish to witness the islands' seasonal changes. This duration enables you to fully immerse yourself in the unique offerings of each time of year.

Visa and Entry Requirements: Navigating Travel Documentation

The Isles of Scilly are part of the United Kingdom. Ensure you check the latest travel regulations, as they may be subject to change. Generally, no visa is required if you're a citizen of the UK, EU, or EEA. However, it's essential to carry a valid form of identification.

For non-UK citizens, check the UK government's official website or consult with the British embassy or consulate in your country to understand visa requirements and entry conditions.

Transportation: Reaching the Isles

Getting to the Isles of Scilly is an adventure; the journey is part of the allure. Explore the following transportation options:

- **Air Travel:** The most common way to reach the Isles is by air. The Isles of Scilly Skybus operates regular flights from Exeter, Newquay, and Land's End airports. The scenic flights provide stunning aerial views before landing on St. Mary's.

- **Ferry Services:** Ferries offer a more leisurely approach if you prefer a slower-paced journey. The Scillonian III ferry sails from Penzance to St. Mary's, providing a picturesque voyage across the Atlantic. It's a fantastic way to witness the islands gradually coming into view.

Both air and ferry services are subject to weather conditions, so it's advisable to check schedules and book in advance, especially during peak seasons.

In conclusion, planning your trip to the Isles of Scilly is a delightful prelude to the await wonders. From choosing the right time to visit to selecting your mode of transportation, each decision contributes to the anticipation and excitement of experiencing this secluded paradise. As you embark on your journey, remember that the Isles of Scilly reward those who approach with a spirit of curiosity and an open heart, ready to embrace the magic of this enchanting archipelago.

Accommodations

Selecting the right accommodation is pivotal to curating your Isles of Scilly experience. The archipelago, with its diverse landscapes and unique island personalities, offers a range of lodging options that cater to various preferences. Whether you seek the comfort of a hotel, the charm of a bed and breakfast, the independence of a self-catering cottage, or the adventurous spirit of camping, the Isles have a haven for every traveler.

Hotels and Resorts: Unveiling Scilly's Luxury

For those desiring a touch of luxury against the backdrop of scenic vistas, hotels, and resorts in the Isles of Scilly provide a refined and comfortable retreat. Here, hospitality meets the untamed beauty of nature:

- **St. Mary's Hall Hotel:** Overlooking Hugh Town, St. Mary's Hall Hotel blends contemporary elegance with traditional charm. Its central location allows easy access to the island's amenities, and the panoramic views from the hotel provide a breathtaking introduction to Scilly.

- **Tresco Island Hotel:** The Tresco Island Hotel stands as the epitome of luxury on the island of Tresco. Surrounded by the subtropical Abbey Gardens, this hotel offers a tranquil escape with spa facilities, fine dining, and access to the island's pristine beaches.

- **Karma St. Martin's Hotel:** For a touch of exclusivity, Karma St. Martin's on St. Martin's island promises a secluded retreat. With stylish accommodations and a focus on wellness, this hotel provides an intimate setting against the backdrop of the azure sea.

Bed and Breakfasts: Personalized Hospitality Amidst Scilly's Charms

For a more intimate and locally immersive experience, bed and breakfasts are scattered across the Isles, offering a warm welcome and personalized hospitality:

- **Star Castle Hotel:** Situated on St. Mary's, the Star Castle Hotel combines history with comfort. Dating back to the 16th century, it offers a unique bed and breakfast experience within the confines of a charming fortress.

- **The Atlantic:** Nestled on the quieter island of St. Mary's, The Atlantic provides a cozy bed and breakfast experience. Guests can enjoy a relaxing stay with tastefully decorated rooms and a friendly atmosphere.

- **Island Home Bed and Breakfast:** Located on Bryher, the Island Home Bed and Breakfast offers a personal touch with only three guest rooms. The owners provide local insights, making it an ideal choice for those seeking an authentic Scillonian experience.

Self-Catering Cottages: Independence Amidst Nature's Bounty

For those who relish the freedom of creating their own Scilly experience, self-catering cottages are scattered across the islands. These accommodations allow you to immerse yourself fully in the archipelago's unique offerings:

- **Hell Bay Hotel Cottages:** On the rugged island of Bryher, Hell Bay Hotel offers self-catering cottages with stunning sea views. Guests can enjoy the freedom of preparing their meals while reveling in the untamed beauty of the surroundings.

- **Churchtown Farm - The Old Farmhouse:** Experience the charm of a historic farmhouse on St. Martin's at Churchtown Farm. The self-catering Old Farmhouse perfectly blends traditional architecture and modern amenities.

- **Carnwethers Country House:** Situated on St. Mary's, Carnwethers Country House offers self-catering accommodations within easy reach of the island's amenities. The well-equipped cottages provide a home-like setting with a touch of Scillonian charm.

Camping Options: Embracing Nature Under Scilly's Stars

For adventurous souls seeking a closer connection to nature, camping options abound on certain islands, allowing you to sleep beneath the Scilly skies:

- **Troytown Campsite:** On the island of St. Agnes, Troytown Campsite offers a picturesque setting overlooking the Atlantic.

With panoramic views and basic facilities, it provides a serene camping experience.

- **Bryher Campsite:** Bryher, the smallest inhabited island, hosts Bryher Campsite, surrounded by heathlands and sandy beaches. Campers can enjoy a rustic experience near the island's natural wonders.

- **St. Martin's Campsite:** St. Martin's Campsite allows campers to immerse themselves in the tranquility of this idyllic island. Easy access to the beaches and walking trails makes it an excellent choice for those seeking a camping adventure.

Choosing Your Scillonian Retreat: Practical Considerations

When selecting your accommodation in the Isles of Scilly, consider the following practicalities:

- **Booking in Advance:** Accommodations can fill up quickly during peak seasons. It's advisable to book well in advance to secure your preferred choice.

- **Location and Accessibility:** Consider the location of your accommodation in relation to your planned activities. Some may prefer central locations for easy access to amenities, while others may seek more secluded options.

- **Facilities and Amenities:** Assess the facilities offered, such as dining options, Wi-Fi, and recreational activities. Self-catering cottages and camping options may have basic amenities, so ensure they align with your preferences.

- **Seasonal Variations:** Some accommodations may have seasonal closures, particularly during winter. Check the availability based on your planned travel dates.

In conclusion, the Isles of Scilly offer various accommodations catering to varied tastes and preferences. Whether you choose the luxury of a hotel, the intimate charm of a bed and breakfast, the independence of a self-catering cottage, or the adventure of camping, each option contributes to the rich tapestry of your Scillonian experience. As you settle into your chosen retreat, you'll find that your accommodation becomes not just a place to stay but an integral part of the enchanting story that unfolds in this captivating archipelago.

Island Overview

The Isles of Scilly, an archipelago adrift in the Atlantic Ocean, beckon with a magnetic charm that lies not only in the collective beauty of the islands but in the distinct character each one possesses. From the bustling St. Mary's to the tranquil shores of St. Agnes and the lesser-known islets of Gugh and Samson, each island contributes a unique chapter to the compelling narrative of Scilly.

Main Islands:

- **St. Mary's: The Archipelago's Beating Heart**

St. Mary's, the largest and most populous of the Isles, is the archipelago's administrative center and primary visitor gateway. Hugh Town, the capital, buzzes with activity, featuring shops, restaurants, and historical sites. The island's landscape is a captivating blend of pristine beaches, heathlands, and rocky cliffs.

Notable Sites:

- The Garrison: A historic fortification with panoramic views of the archipelago.

- St. Mary's Museum: Uncover the island's rich history through exhibits and artifacts.

- **Tresco: A Subtropical Paradise**

Tresco, the second-largest island, offers a subtropical haven with the world-renowned Abbey Gardens at its heart. Exotic flora thrives in this unique microclimate, creating a lush tapestry against sandy beaches. The island's serene ambiance invites relaxation and exploration.

Notable Sites:

- Abbey Gardens: Home to over 20,000 species of plants worldwide.

- Tresco Abbey: Explore the ruins of an Augustinian priory.

- **St. Martin's: Tranquility Personified**

St. Martin's, known for its peaceful ambiance, boasts white sandy beaches and crystal-clear waters. The island is a haven for walkers and nature enthusiasts, with a network of footpaths offering breathtaking views. St. Martin's encapsulates the essence of a secluded retreat.

Notable Sites:

- Daymark: A distinctive navigation tower providing panoramic views.

- St. Martin's Vineyard: Discover a local winemaking tradition.

- **Bryher: Rugged Beauty and Secluded Bliss**

The smallest of the inhabited islands, Bryher, captivates with its rugged landscapes and secluded coves. Popular among nature lovers and hikers, Bryher's untamed beauty invites exploration, from coastal trails to panoramic viewpoints.

Notable Sites:

- Hell Bay: A picturesque bay renowned for its dramatic scenery.

- Fraggle Rock Bar: Unwind with a drink at this laid-back island bar.

- **St. Agnes: A Remote Paradise**

St. Agnes, the southernmost inhabited island, exudes tranquility and remoteness. With a population of around 70 people, St. Agnes offers a serene escape with sandy beaches, scenic walks, and opportunities for birdwatching.

Notable Sites:

- Turk's Head: A distinctive rock formation on the island's western coast.

- Troytown Farm: Sample local ice cream and enjoy views of the Atlantic.

Lesser-Known Islands:

- **Gugh: A Hidden Gem**

Gugh is a hidden gem awaiting discovery, connected to St. Agnes by a sandbar. With its small population and unspoiled landscapes, Gugh offers a peaceful retreat and stunning views of the surrounding islands.

Notable Sites:

- Old Blockhouse: Explore the remnants of a historic defensive structure.

- St. Agnes and Gugh Bar: Walk between the islands at low tide.

- **Samson: Nature's Sanctuary**

Once inhabited but now uninhabited, Samson stands as a natural sanctuary with a rich history. Nature has reclaimed this island, creating a haven for wildlife and a sense of solitude for those who venture to its shores.

Notable Sites:

- Cromwell's Castle: A historical fortress with views of the surrounding islands.

- Ancient Settlement: Discover the remnants of prehistoric structures.

Choosing Your Island Experience: Practical Considerations

- **Transportation Between Islands:** Inter-island transportation is primarily by boat. Scheduled boat services connect the main islands, and private boat hires are available for a more personalized experience.

- **Accommodations:** Each island offers a range of accommodations, from hotels and bed and breakfasts to self-catering cottages. Consider the atmosphere and amenities that align with your preferences.

- **Activities:** Tailor your visit based on the activities each island offers. St. Mary's provides a hub of cultural and historical sites. At the same time, the smaller islands offer opportunities for outdoor adventures and serene relaxation.

- **Weather Considerations:** The Isles of Scilly enjoy a mild maritime climate, but weather conditions vary. Pack accordingly, and check local forecasts for each island to plan your activities.

In conclusion, the Isles of Scilly unfold as a mosaic of unique islands, each with its allure and personality. Whether you seek the bustling energy of St. Mary's, the subtropical gardens of Tresco, the tranquil retreat of St. Martin's, the rugged beauty of Bryher, or the remote paradise of St. Agnes, the archipelago promises an unforgettable journey.

Venture beyond the well-trodden paths to discover the lesser-known islands of Gugh and Samson, where nature and history intertwine. As you navigate this enchanting archipelago, each island becomes a chapter in your own Scillonian story, a tale of discovery, serenity, and the timeless beauty of the Isles of Scilly.

Activities and Attractions

The Isles of Scilly, with their breathtaking landscapes and rich cultural heritage, offer a tapestry of activities and attractions catering to diverse interests. From exploring historical sites that whisper tales of the past to embarking on outdoor adventures that connect you with the archipelago's natural wonders, the Isles invites you to immerse yourself in a captivating blend of history, exploration, and cultural festivities.

Historical Sites: Echoes of Centuries Past

- **Cromwell's Castle on Tresco:** Overlooking New Grimsby Harbor on Tresco, Cromwell's Castle is a testament to the archipelago's maritime history. Built during the English Civil War, this fortress provides panoramic views of the surrounding islands. It offers a glimpse into the strategic importance of the Isles.

- **Star Castle on St. Mary's:** An iconic fortress on St. Mary's, the Star Castle dates back to the 16th century. Originally built as a defensive structure against pirate raids, it now serves as a unique hotel. Explore its historic rooms and ramparts and absorb the tales of battles and sieges that echo through its walls.

- **King Charles's Castle on Tresco:** Perched on the hill overlooking Old Grimsby Harbor, King Charles's Castle is a ruin that harks back to the Civil War era. While the castle is in disrepair, its views of Tresco and beyond are worth the hike.

Outdoor Adventures: Exploring Scilly's Natural Wonders

- **Coastal Walks on St. Agnes:** St. Agnes, with its rugged coastline and secluded coves, is a haven for coastal walks. Embark on the Circular Walk, offering breathtaking views of the Atlantic, or explore the Beady Pool and Covean trails, where dramatic cliffs meet the turquoise sea.

- **Bryher's Hell Bay Coastal Path:** The Hell Bay Coastal Path on Bryher unfolds a spectacular route along the island's western coast. Traverse heathlands, sandy beaches, and rocky cliffs, encountering unparalleled vistas and the untamed beauty of Bryher.

- **Gugh and the Sandbar Walk:** Gugh, connected to St. Agnes by a sandbar, provides an opportunity for an exhilarating walk between the two islands at low tide. Experience the unique sensation of walking across the Atlantic Ocean, surrounded by stunning coastal landscapes.

Hiking Trails: A Scenic Exploration

- **St. Martin's Daymark Trail:** St. Martin's offers the Daymark Trail, a circular route that leads to the Daymark Tower. This distinctive navigation tower provides panoramic views of the islands and offers a picturesque setting for a leisurely hike.

- **Tresco Abbey Gardens Walk:** Explore the diverse landscapes of Tresco with a walk through the renowned Abbey Gardens. Meander through subtropical plants, vibrant blooms, and serene pathways, enjoying the tranquil ambiance of this botanical haven.

- **St. Mary's Garrison and Old Town Trail:** St. Mary's boasts the Garrison and Old Town Trail, guiding you through historic sites, ancient burial chambers, and scenic viewpoints. The trail offers a blend of history and nature, making it a rewarding hike for enthusiasts of both.

Water Sports: Embracing the Maritime Spirit

- **Snorkeling in the Crystal-Clear Waters:** The crystal-clear waters surrounding the Isles of Scilly invite snorkelers to discover vibrant marine life and underwater landscapes. Porthcressa Beach on St. Mary's and Green Bay on Bryher are popular spots for snorkeling adventures.

- **Kayaking around St. Agnes:** Explore the coastal beauty of St. Agnes by kayaking around its shores. Paddle through clear waters, discovering hidden coves and sea caves. Kayak rentals and guided tours are available for both beginners and experienced kayakers.

- **Scuba Diving in Scillonian Waters:** For experienced divers, the Scillonian waters offer a unique underwater realm to explore.

Dive sites around the islands reveal shipwrecks, vibrant marine ecosystems, and the diverse sea life in this maritime haven.

Wildlife Watching: Nature's Extravaganza

- **Birdwatching on St. Mary's and St. Agnes:** The Isles of Scilly are a paradise for birdwatchers, especially during migration seasons. St. Mary's and St. Agnes are known for their diverse bird populations. Look for puffins, seals, and various seabirds along the coastal cliffs.

- **Seal-Watching Tours:** Embark on a seal-watching tour around the islands to witness these playful creatures in their natural habitat. Boat excursions offer a chance to see seals basking on rocks and playing in the surrounding waters.

- **Wildlife Safaris on Tresco:** Tresco organizes wildlife safaris that take you to hidden corners of the island, showcasing its diverse flora and fauna. Spot red squirrels, seals, and a variety of bird species as you explore the landscapes of this unique island.

Cultural Events and Festivals: Celebrating Scilly's Spirit

- **Tresco Abbey Gardens' Events:** Tresco Abbey Gardens hosts various cultural events, from outdoor concerts to garden parties. These events provide a unique opportunity to experience the cultural richness of the Isles while surrounded by the beauty of the gardens.

- **Low Tide Day on Bryher:** Bryher's Low Tide Day is a local celebration when the tide is low enough to reveal a sandbar connecting Bryher and Tresco. The community comes together for festivities, including live music, food, and traditional games.

- **Regatta Week on St. Mary's:** St. Mary's Regatta Week is a highlight of the summer calendar. This lively event features boat races, live music, and a carnival atmosphere, bringing locals and visitors together to celebrate the maritime spirit of the Isles.

Planning Your Isles of Scilly Adventure: Practical Considerations

- **Seasonal Considerations:** Some activities and events may be seasonal, so it's advisable to check the timing of your visit to coincide with specific attractions or festivals.

- **Guided Tours:** Consider joining guided tours or excursions to maximize your activities. Local guides often provide insights into the natural and cultural history of the islands.

- **Equipment Rentals:** Check for equipment rental services for water sports and outdoor activities. Many providers offer kayaks, snorkeling gear, and bikes for exploration.

- **Weather Awareness:** The weather in the Isles of Scilly can be changeable. Dress in layers and be prepared for occasional rain. Check local forecasts before embarking on outdoor activities.

In conclusion, the Isles of Scilly invite you to embark on a journey of exploration and cultural enrichment. Whether you're drawn to the historical sites that echo centuries of stories, the outdoor adventures that connect you with nature's wonders, or the vibrant cultural events that celebrate Scilly's spirit, each activity unfolds a new facet of this enchanting archipelago. As you plan your Isles of Scilly adventure, remember that the true magic lies in the destinations you explore and the experiences you gather, creating memories that linger long after you've left these captivating shores.

Dining and Cuisine

The culinary scene in the Isles of Scilly reflects the archipelago's unique blend of maritime heritage, local produce, and a commitment to sustainability. From savoring fresh seafood caught in the surrounding waters to indulging in traditional Scillonian dishes, the dining experience in Scilly is a journey into flavors that mirror the pristine beauty of the islands.

Local Cuisine: Unveiling Scilly's Culinary Treasures

- **Fresh Seafood:** With the azure waters of the Atlantic Ocean at their doorstep, the Isles of Scilly are a seafood lover's paradise. Indulge in the day's catch, from succulent lobster and crab to plump scallops and seasonal fish. Many restaurants and eateries source their seafood locally, ensuring a fresh and delectable dining experience.

- **Scillonian Crab:** A culinary gem celebrated for its sweet, delicate flavor. Often served with minimal seasoning to let the natural taste shine, crab dishes range from crab salads to creamy crab bisques.

- **Local Produce:** Embracing a farm-to-table ethos, the Isles of Scilly take pride in their local produce. Fresh vegetables, herbs, and fruits are cultivated on the islands, contributing to the vibrant and seasonal offerings on the dining table.

Recommended Restaurants: A Culinary Exploration

- **Juliet's Garden Restaurant (St. Mary's):** Nestled on the edge of Old Town Bay on St. Mary's, Juliet's Garden Restaurant offers a picturesque setting and a diverse menu showcasing local produce and seafood. Enjoy alfresco dining on the terrace, surrounded by lush gardens and panoramic sea views.

- **The New Inn (Tresco):** Located on Tresco, The New Inn combines a cozy pub atmosphere with a menu featuring locally sourced ingredients. From hearty pub classics to seafood specialties, this establishment provides a taste of Scilly's culinary offerings.

- **Fraggle Rock Bar (Bryher):** Overlooking the stunning Hell Bay on Bryher, Fraggle Rock Bar provides a laid-back and welcoming atmosphere. Sample their seafood platters or enjoy a drink while soaking in the breathtaking views of the rugged coastline.

- **Karma St. Martin's (St. Martin's):** Karma St. Martin's offers luxurious accommodations and boasts a restaurant emphasizing fresh, seasonal, and locally sourced ingredients. Dine elegantly while enjoying dishes showcasing the best of Scilly's produce.

- **Tregarthen's Hotel Restaurant (St. Mary's):** Situated in the heart of Hugh Town on St. Mary's, Tregarthen's Hotel Restaurant provides a refined dining experience with a menu inspired by local and international flavors. The restaurant's panoramic windows offer views of the bustling harbor.

Traditional Pubs and Bars: A Toast to Scilly's Spirit

- **The Atlantic Inn (St. Mary's):** As one of the oldest inns on the islands, The Atlantic Inn exudes charm and character. The pub serves traditional pub fare with a focus on local ingredients, and the welcoming atmosphere makes it a popular choice for locals and visitors alike.

- **Seven Stones Inn (St. Martin's):** Located on St. Martin's, the Seven Stones Inn is a traditional pub offering a relaxed setting. With a selection of local ales and a menu featuring pub classics, it provides a cozy spot to unwind after a day of exploration.

- **The Turks Head (St. Agnes):** Overlooking the quay on St. Agnes, The Turks Head is a quintessential island pub with a welcoming ambiance. Enjoy a drink from their well-stocked bar or savor a meal featuring locally sourced ingredients.

- **Bishop and Wolf (St. Mary's):** Situated in Hugh Town on St. Mary's, the Bishop and Wolf combines the atmosphere of a traditional pub with a modern touch. The pub serves various dishes, including seafood specials and classic pub favorites.

Savoring Scilly: Practical Considerations

- **Dining Reservations:** While the Isles of Scilly exude a laid-back atmosphere, making reservations is advisable, especially during peak seasons or for popular dining establishments. This ensures you secure a table at your preferred time.

- **Seasonal Variations:** Remember that some restaurants may have seasonal closures or varying opening hours. Check ahead, especially if you have specific dining preferences during your visit.

- **Local Specialties:** Take advantage of the opportunity to try local specialties and seafood dishes that capture the essence of Scilly's culinary heritage. Ask for local recommendations or explore menus showcasing the best of the islands' flavors.

- **Bar and Pub Etiquette:** In traditional pubs and bars, embrace the friendly island spirit by conversing with locals and fellow visitors. Enjoy the laid-back atmosphere, and don't hesitate to ask for local drinks and dish recommendations.

In conclusion, dining on the Isles of Scilly celebrates coastal living, where the sea's bounty meets the richness of the islands' produce. From savoring fresh seafood in acclaimed restaurants to embracing the warmth of traditional pubs, each dining experience in Scilly unfolds as a chapter in the archipelago's gastronomic story. As you raise a glass to the panoramic sea views or savor a dish crafted from local ingredients, you'll find that dining in Scilly is about nourishing the body and immersing yourself in the soulful flavors of this captivating island paradise.

Sample Itineraries

The Isles of Scilly, with their diverse landscapes, rich history, and vibrant culture, offer a myriad of experiences for every traveler. Whether you're seeking a relaxing weekend escape, planning a family-friendly vacation, craving a nature and adventure expedition, or eager for a historical and cultural discovery, the Isles of Scilly provide the perfect backdrop for an unforgettable journey. Let these sample itineraries serve as guides to help you craft your unique Scillonian adventure.

1. Weekend Escape to the Isles of Scilly: Unwind in Tranquil Beauty

Friday: Arrival and Sunset Stroll

- Arrive on St. Mary's, the largest island, via the Skybus or Scillonian ferry.

- Check into a charming bed and breakfast or a boutique hotel like Juliet's Garden Restaurant for a tranquil stay.

- Take a stroll along Porthcressa Beach and savor the sunset views.

Saturday: Island Exploration and Relaxation

- Explore St. Mary's historical sites, including the Star Castle and the Garrison, absorbing the island's maritime history.

- Enjoy a fresh seafood lunch at a local eatery like Juliet's Garden Restaurant.

- Afternoon relaxation at Porthcressa Beach or the subtropical Tresco Abbey Gardens.

- Dine at a seaside restaurant, savoring the flavors of Scilly's local cuisine.

Sunday: Island-Hopping Adventure

- Take a boat to St. Agnes, the southernmost inhabited island.

- Discover the secluded coves and beaches, including Beady Pool and Covean.

- Savor a meal at a traditional pub like The Turks Head.

- Return to St. Mary's in the evening, capturing the sunset over the Atlantic.

2. Family-Friendly Vacation: Delight in Scilly's Natural Wonders

Monday: Arrival and Island Orientation

- Arrive at St. Mary's with the family, settling into family-friendly accommodation like a self-catering cottage.

- Explore the town, introducing the kids to the local charm of Hugh Town.

- Enjoy a family dinner at a welcoming restaurant with options for all ages.

Tuesday: Tresco Adventure Day

- Take the boat to Tresco and explore the world-famous Abbey Gardens, a delight for nature-loving families.

- Picnic amidst the subtropical blooms or dine at The New Inn for a family-friendly meal.

- Visit the Valhalla Museum to discover ship figureheads and maritime history.

Wednesday: Bryher Excursion

- Embark on a boat trip to Bryher, the smallest inhabited island.

- Hike the Hell Bay Coastal Path for family-friendly walks and scenic views.

- Enjoy a beach day at the picturesque Rushy Bay.

- Dine at Fraggle Rock Bar for a relaxed family dinner.

Thursday: St. Martin's Serenity

- Venture to St. Martin's, known for its tranquil ambiance.

- Explore the Daymark Trail with the family, offering panoramic views.

- Relax on Par Beach and let the kids play in the shallow waters.

- For a family-friendly setting, have dinner at a local eatery, perhaps Karma St. Martin's.

Friday: Departure with Last-Minute Explorations

- Before departing, explore the local markets for unique souvenirs and treats.

- Take a final stroll along one of the scenic coastal paths.

- Depart with family memories filled with nature, adventure, and the warmth of the Isles.

3. Nature and Adventure Expedition: Thrills Amidst Scilly's Beauty

Monday: Arrival and Coastal Exploration

- Arrive at St. Mary's and check into a self-catering cottage for an independent adventure.

- Begin with a coastal exploration, walking the Garrison and enjoying the panoramic views.

- Dinner at a local pub or restaurant focusing on fresh, locally sourced ingredients.

Tuesday: Water Adventures and Seal Watching

- Engage in water sports such as kayaking or snorkeling around St. Agnes.

- Join a seal-watching tour to witness these playful creatures in their natural habitat.

- Dinner at a seaside restaurant, indulging in the day's aquatic adventures.

Wednesday: Bryher's Rugged Beauty

- Take a boat to Bryher and hike the rugged Hell Bay Coastal Path.

- Enjoy a picnic on the cliffs, taking in the untamed beauty of Bryher.

- Head to Fraggle Rock Bar for a hearty meal and a relaxing atmosphere.

Thursday: St. Martin's Daymark Trail

- Explore St. Martin's, hiking the Daymark Trail for breathtaking views.

- Take a break at the island's vineyard, sampling local wines.

- Opt for a sunset dinner at Karma St. Martin's, soaking in the serene ambiance.

Friday: Tresco's Subtropical Paradise

- Spend the day on Tresco, exploring the Abbey Gardens and its unique flora.

- Participate in a wildlife safari to discover Tresco's diverse ecosystems.

- Dine at The New Inn, recounting the day's adventures.

4. Historical and Cultural Discovery: Unveiling Scilly's Heritage

Monday: Arrival and Historical St. Mary's

- Arrive at St. Mary's and check into a historic hotel like Star Castle.

- Explore the historic sites of St. Mary's, including the Star Castle and the Old Town.

- Dine at a restaurant with a blend of local and international flavors.

Tuesday: Tresco's Maritime Legacy

- Venture to Tresco and explore the Valhalla Museum, showcasing maritime history.

- Visit Tresco Abbey, unraveling the island's monastic past.

- Lunch at a traditional inn, enjoying classic British fare.

Wednesday: Bryher's Ancient Sites

- Take a boat to Bryher and visit ancient sites, including the Hell Bay Hotel.

- Explore the remains of the Old Blockhouse, a historic defensive structure.

- Dinner at Fraggle Rock Bar, soaking in the island's timeless charm.

Thursday: St. Agnes' Secluded Heritage

- Discover St. Agnes, exploring the historic Turk's Head and Troytown Farm.

- Visit the island's museum, delving into its unique history.

- Dinner at a traditional pub, experiencing the local hospitality.

Friday: Departure with Cultural Insights

- Before departing, visit local art galleries and craft shops for cultural souvenirs.

- Attend any ongoing cultural events or festivals.

- Depart with a rich tapestry of Scillonian history and cultural experiences.

Planning Your Scillonian Adventure: Practical Considerations

- **Transportation:** Check ferry and flight schedules in advance, especially during peak seasons. Book tickets and transfers accordingly.

- **Accommodations:** Choose accommodations based on your itinerary and preferences—book in advance, especially for popular stays.

- **Weather Awareness:** Pack layers and check the weather forecast, as it can be changeable. Be prepared for occasional rain.

- **Activity Reservations:** If participating in guided tours or specific activities, consider making reservations in advance.

- **Local Events:** Check for local events, festivals, or cultural happenings during your visit to enhance your Scillonian experience.

In crafting your Isles of Scilly itinerary, remember that the archipelago's magic lies in the balance of exploration and relaxation. Whether you're drawn to the historical tales, the natural wonders, or the cultural vibrancy, the Isles of Scilly offer a canvas for a personalized journey that will linger in your memories long after you've bid farewell to these enchanting shores.

Practical Tips and Information

Embarking to the Isles of Scilly promises an enchanting escape to natural beauty, historical charm, and cultural richness. To ensure a seamless and enjoyable experience, it's essential to consider practical aspects such as packing essentials, currency and payment methods, local customs and etiquette, health and safety precautions, and useful phrases to navigate the friendly island atmosphere. Here's a comprehensive guide for your Isles of Scilly adventure.

Packing Essentials: Preparedness for Island Living

1. **Weather-Appropriate Clothing:** The Isles of Scilly experience a mild maritime climate, but the weather can be changeable—pack layers, including waterproof jackets, comfortable walking shoes, and breathable clothing for outdoor explorations.

2. **Swimwear and Snorkeling Gear:** Given the pristine beaches and crystal-clear waters, remember to pack swimwear and, if

you're inclined, snorkeling gear to explore the underwater wonders around the islands.

3. **Daypack and Outdoor Essentials:** Bring a daypack for your island explorations, with sunscreen, a hat, water bottles, and insect repellent. If you plan on hiking, consider packing a compact first aid kit.

4. **Travel Adapters:** Ensure you have the appropriate travel adapters to charge your devices. The Isles of Scilly use the UK standard power outlets.

5. **Binoculars and Camera:** Capture the islands' stunning landscapes and unique wildlife with a camera. Binoculars are also handy for birdwatching and enjoying the scenic views.

6. **Reusable Water Bottle and Eco-Friendly Items:** Support the islands' commitment to sustainability by bringing a reusable water bottle. Consider eco-friendly items such as a reusable shopping bag to reduce single-use plastic waste.

7. **Local Guidebook and Maps:** Carry a local guidebook to learn about the history

and attractions of the Isles of Scilly. Maps or navigation apps will help you explore the islands on foot or by bike.

Currency and Payment Methods: Navigating Financial Transactions

1. **Currency:** The currency used in the Isles of Scilly is the British Pound Sterling (GBP). Ensure you have sufficient cash for small purchases, as not all establishments may accept cards.

2. **Payment Methods:** While major credit and debit cards are generally accepted, carrying some cash is advisable, especially on smaller islands or when visiting local markets. Check with your accommodation and local businesses about their preferred payment methods.

3. **ATMs:** ATMs are available at St. Mary's and Tresco, providing a convenient way to withdraw cash. However, services may be limited on smaller islands, so plan accordingly.

4. **Tipping Etiquette:** Tipping is customary in restaurants and for services. While it's not obligatory, leaving a tip for good service is appreciated. Check if a service charge is included in your bill before adding a tip.

Local Customs and Etiquette: Embracing Scillonian Hospitality

1. **Island Time:** The pace of life in the Isles of Scilly is relaxed, and locals operate on "island time." Embrace the laid-back atmosphere, and don't be in a hurry. Patience is a virtue in this tranquil archipelago.

2. **Friendliness and Courtesy:** Islanders are known for their friendliness and warmth. Greetings are important; a simple "hello" or "good morning" goes a long way. Engage in friendly conversations with locals, who are often eager to share their island insights.

3. **Respecting Nature:** The islands' delicate ecosystems and pristine landscapes are crucial to their charm. Respect nature by staying on marked paths, avoiding

disturbance to wildlife, and following any environmental guidelines provided.

4. **Photography Etiquette:** If taking photographs of locals, seek permission first. Respect private property and avoid intrusive photography, especially in residential areas.

5. **Cultural Events and Festivals:** If your visit coincides with a local event or festival, join in the celebrations with respect. These events offer an excellent opportunity to immerse yourself in Scillonian culture.

Health and Safety: Ensuring Well-Being During Your Stay

1. **Healthcare Services:** St. Mary's has a hospital and medical facilities. However, consider bringing a basic first aid kit for minor ailments or injuries. If you have specific medical needs, inform your accommodation in advance.

2. **Travel Insurance:** Ensure you have comprehensive travel insurance that covers medical emergencies, trip cancellations, and other unforeseen circumstances. Check if

your insurance includes coverage for outdoor activities or water sports.

3. **Emergency Services:** The emergency number in the UK, including the Isles of Scilly, is 999. For non-emergency medical assistance at St. Mary's, you can contact the St. Mary's Health Centre.

4. **Water Safety:** If engaging in water activities, follow safety guidelines and be aware of local conditions. Check weather forecasts, wear appropriate gear, and, if needed, enlist the services of experienced guides for water excursions.

Useful Phrases: Connecting with Locals Through Language

1. **Greetings:**

    - Hello: "Hello" or "Hi"

    - Good morning: "Good morning"

    - Good evening: "Good evening"

    - Goodbye: "Goodbye" or "Cheerio"

2. **Courtesy Phrases:**

  - Please: "Please"

  - Thank you: "Thank you" or "Thanks"

  - Excuse me: "Excuse me" or "Pardon"

3. **Getting Around:**

  - Where is...?: "Where is...?"

  - How do I get to...?: "How do I get to...?"

  - Can you help me?: "Can you help me?"

4. **Dining Etiquette:**

  - Menu: "Menu"

  - Water: "Water"

  - Bill, please: "Can I have the bill, please?"

5. **Emergencies:**

  - Help: "Help"

  - Emergency: "Emergency"

  - I need a doctor: "I need a doctor

6. **Island-Specific Phrases:**

- Scillonian: "Scillonian"

- Isles of Scilly: "Isles of Scilly"

- Islander: "Islander"

Navigating the Isles with Ease: Final Considerations

- **Local Information Centers:** Visit local information centers in St. Mary's for additional guidance, maps, and updates on events or activities.

- **Transportation Reservations:** If planning inter-island travel, consider booking transportation in advance, especially during peak seasons.

- **Weather Updates:** Stay informed about weather conditions, as they can impact outdoor activities. Check local forecasts regularly.

- **Island Events and Festivals:** Explore local events and festivals during your Stay. These celebrations offer insights into the

Isles of Scilly's community spirit and cultural richness.

As you prepare for your Isles of Scilly adventure, remember that the islands' true allure lies in their welcoming atmosphere, natural wonders, and the genuine hospitality of the locals. By embracing the practical tips and information provided, you'll be well-equipped to navigate the charming landscapes and create lasting memories in this idyllic corner of the world. Have a safe trip, and enjoy your Scillonian journey!

Getting Around

The Isles of Scilly, an archipelago off the southwestern tip of Cornwall, beckon with their pristine landscapes and scattered isles. Getting around this enchanting destination involves a delightful mix of inter-island transportation, where boats weave through azure waters, and the unhurried pace of bicycling and walking allows you to savor the islands' natural beauty at your own pace.

Inter-Island Transportation: Connecting Isles of Wonder

The Scillonian III: A Maritime Gateway

Embarking on your Scillonian adventure often begins with a scenic voyage aboard the Scillonian III. This passenger ferry, connecting Penzance on the Cornish mainland to St. Mary's, serves as a maritime gateway to the archipelago. The journey across the Atlantic takes approximately 2 hours and 45 minutes, offering breathtaking views of the open sea and the emerging outlines of the Isles of Scilly.

Skybus: Wings Over Azure Waters

The Skybus provides an aerial perspective on the islands' beauty for a swifter arrival. Operating flights from Land's End Airport and Newquay Airport, the Skybus lands at St. Mary's, providing an efficient mode of transportation. The short flight offers panoramic views of the islands, adding an extra layer of awe to your journey.

Inter-Island Boats: Seafaring Adventures

Navigating between the individual islands is a key part of the Scillonian experience. Various boat services, including the St. Mary's Boatmen's Association and Tresco Boats, connect the main islands and some lesser-known gems. Each boat journey from bustling St. Mary's to serene St. Agnes unveils a new facet of the archipelago's charm.

Tips for Inter-Island Transportation:

- **Check Schedules:** Verify ferry and boat schedules in advance, especially during peak seasons. Schedules may vary based on weather conditions.

- **Reservations:** Consider making reservations for ferry services, especially if you have a tight itinerary or plan to travel during popular times.

- **Weather Awareness:** Be mindful of the weather, as sea conditions can influence boat services. Check weather forecasts regularly, and stay informed about any potential disruptions.

- **Carrying Luggage:** Be prepared to manage your luggage, as some boats have limited space. Pack efficiently and consider bringing a small, easily manageable suitcase or backpack.

Bicycling and Walking: Embracing the Isles at a Leisurely Pace

Island Exploration by Bike:

Bicycling is a favored mode of transportation on the Isles of Scilly, offering a leisurely and eco-friendly way to explore the islands. Renting a bicycle is convenient, with rental services at St. Mary's and Tresco. The flat terrain and well-maintained paths make cycling accessible for visitors of all ages and fitness levels.

Walking Paths and Trails:

Walking unveils the islands' hidden treasures for those seeking a slower pace. St. Mary's alone boasts an extensive network of walking paths, from coastal trails to historic routes. Notable trails include the Garrison and Old Town Trail, revealing ancient burial chambers and panoramic viewpoints, and the Higher Moors and Lower Moors Trail, providing a glimpse into Scilly's diverse flora and fauna.

Bicycling and Walking on Tresco:

Tresco, the second-largest island, is a paradise for cyclists and walkers alike. With no private cars allowed, the island encourages exploration by foot or bike. The Tresco Abbey Gardens, a botanical haven, is easily accessible, and cycling along the coastal roads reveals breathtaking seascapes.

Guidelines for Bicycling and Walking:

- **Trail Maps:** Obtain trail maps from local information centers or accommodation providers. Maps outline walking routes, cycling paths, and points of interest.

- **Rental Services:** Rent bicycles from local providers and inquire about any guided walks or group activities available during your visit.

- **Island-Specific Rules:** Familiarize yourself with any island-specific rules for cycling and walking. For example, some areas may be designated as nature reserves with specific guidelines.

- **Weather-Appropriate Gear:** Pack weather-appropriate gear for cycling and walking, including comfortable footwear, sunscreen, and a light jacket. The weather on the islands can be changeable, so it's advisable to dress in layers.

Integration of Transportation Modes: A Seamless Journey

A notable aspect of exploring the Isles of Scilly is the seamless integration of transportation modes. Start your day with a leisurely bike ride along St. Mary's coastal paths, pausing for panoramic views. As the day unfolds, embark on a boat journey to a neighboring island, where you can stroll along pristine beaches or explore historical sites. Integrating walking, cycling, and boating allows for an immersive and flexible archipelago exploration.

Cultural Considerations: Adapting to Island Living

While traversing the Isles of Scilly, it's essential to adapt to the unhurried pace and island etiquette:

- **Respect Nature:** Stay on designated paths to preserve the islands' delicate ecosystems. Avoid disturbing wildlife, and follow any environmental guidelines provided.

- **Island Time:** Embrace the local rhythm of life, known as "island time." This relaxed approach encourages visitors to savor the moment and appreciate the beauty around them.

- **Friendly Interactions:** Interact with locals, whether asking for directions or conversing at a local pub. The warmth of the community adds to the richness of your Scillonian experience.

The Isles of Scilly beckons with an invitation to explore their wonders, and getting around becomes an integral part of the adventure. From the maritime tales woven by boat journeys to the unhurried pace of cycling and walking, each mode of transportation contributes to the enchantment of the archipelago. Whether you choose the panoramic views from the Scillonian III, the aerial perspective of the Skybus, the island-hopping boat adventures, or the tranquil exploration by bike and foot, your journey through the Isles of Scilly promises an odyssey filled with natural beauty, cultural richness, and memories that linger like the sea breeze.

Isles of Scilly for Special Interests

The Isles of Scilly, a haven of natural beauty and cultural richness, offer a bespoke adventure for those with special interests. Whether you're a birdwatching enthusiast, a photography aficionado, or someone eager to unleash their artistic talents, the archipelago caters to diverse passions. Immerse yourself in a birdwatching paradise, capture breathtaking moments through photography, or participate in art and craft workshops that tap into the creative spirit of the islands.

Birdwatching Paradise: A Symphony of Feathers and Flight

The Isles of Scilly, situated on major bird migration routes, are a birdwatcher's paradise. With diverse habitats, including coastal cliffs, heathlands, and wetlands, the archipelago attracts a remarkable array of bird species throughout the year. From the distinctive call of seabirds to the vibrant plumage of migratory species, Scilly unfolds as a natural symphony for birdwatching enthusiasts.

Key Birdwatching Hotspots:

1. **St. Mary's:** Explore the Garrison and Peninnis Head for sightings of seabirds, including puffins, razorbills, and guillemots. The pools and wetlands provide opportunities to observe wading birds.

2. **St. Agnes and Gugh:** These islands are home to breeding colonies of seabirds, including gulls and fulmars. The rocky shores and coastal paths offer ideal vantage points for birdwatching.

3. **Bryher:** Head to Shipman Head Down for panoramic views, where you might spot birds of prey like kestrels and peregrine falcons. The island's diverse landscapes attract a variety of birdlife.

4. **Tresco:** Visit Tresco Abbey Gardens, a botanical paradise attracting residents and migratory birds. The garden's diverse flora provides a haven for songbirds and other species.

Tips for Birdwatching:

- **Binoculars and Field Guides:** Bring a pair of binoculars for close-up views of birds, and consider carrying a field guide to identify species. Local guidebooks may provide insights into birdwatching hotspots.

- **Seasonal Variations:** Different seasons bring different bird species to the Isles of Scilly. Research the best times for specific sightings, whether it's the nesting season or the arrival of migratory birds.

- **Guided Tours:** Consider joining guided birdwatching tours led by local experts. They can provide valuable insights, share knowledge about bird behavior, and help you spot elusive species.

Photography Opportunities: Capturing Scilly's Essence Frame by Frame

For photography enthusiasts, the Isles of Scilly is a canvas of inspiration, offering an array of landscapes, seascapes, and cultural vignettes to capture. From golden sunsets casting a warm glow on tranquil beaches to rugged cliffs and historic sites, the archipelago beckons photographers to frame its essence through their lenses.

Key Photography Locations:

1. **Old Town, St. Mary's:** Explore Old Town's historic charm with its iconic buildings, ancient church, and the captivating Porth Hellick Beach. The golden hour lends a magical quality to this area, perfect for capturing the play of light and shadow.

2. **Tresco Abbey Gardens:** This botanical paradise is not only a treat for nature lovers but also a haven for photographers. Capture the vibrant colors of exotic blooms, intricate details of plant life, and the play of light filtering through the garden.

3. **St. Agnes Lighthouse:** Perched on the rugged cliffs of St. Agnes, the lighthouse provides a striking backdrop for dramatic seascapes. The interplay of waves crashing against the rocks and the coastal scenery offers excellent photo opportunities.

4. **Bryher's Hell Bay:** The wild beauty of Hell Bay on Bryher is a magnet for photographers. The rugged coastline,

weathered rocks, and expansive views of the Atlantic Ocean provide a captivating setting for coastal photography.

Photography Tips:

- **Golden Hour Magic:** Take advantage of the golden hour, shortly after sunrise or before sunset, when the light is soft and warm. This is an ideal time to capture the islands in a magical glow.

- **Varied Perspectives:** Experiment with different perspectives, from capturing wide-angle landscapes to zooming in on intricate details. The diverse scenery of the Isles of Scilly lends itself to a range of photographic styles.

- **Weather Adaptation:** Be prepared for changeable weather conditions. Embrace the opportunity to capture dramatic cloud formations, rainbows, or misty landscapes. Pack weather-resistant gear to protect your equipment.

- **Cultural Moments:** Engage with the local community and capture cultural moments, whether it's a traditional event, a bustling market, or the warm smiles of islanders.

These candid shots add depth to your Scillonian photo story.

Art and Craft Workshops: Unleashing Creativity in Island Ambiance

The artistic spirit of the Isles of Scilly extends beyond its natural beauty, welcoming individuals to engage in art and craft workshops that draw inspiration from the surroundings. Whether you're a seasoned artist or a novice eager to explore your creative side, the islands offer a range of opportunities to immerse yourself in artistic expression.

Artistic Endeavors on St. Mary's:

1. **Gallery Tresco:** Located on St. Mary's, Gallery Tresco showcases a diverse collection of contemporary art, including paintings, sculptures, and ceramics. Workshops and artist talks are occasionally hosted, providing insights into creative processes.

2. **St. Mary's Hall Hotel Art Studio:** This hotel on St. Mary's boasts an art studio where guests can participate in workshops

led by local artists. From painting to pottery, the studio offers a space for creative exploration.

Crafting Experiences on Tresco:

1. **Tresco Abbey Gardens Workshops:** Tresco Abbey Gardens occasionally hosts art and craft workshops amidst its lush surroundings. From botanical illustration to nature-inspired crafts, these workshops fuse creativity with the beauty of the gardens.

Tips for Art and Craft Workshops:

- **Advance Booking:** If you're interested in participating in workshops, especially those with limited slots, consider booking in advance. Check with local galleries, studios, or cultural centers for upcoming events.

- **Explore Local Art Galleries:** Visit local art galleries and studios to discover the works of Scillonian artists. Engage with the art community, attend exhibitions, and inquire about ongoing workshops or classes.

- **Outdoor Sketching:** Take advantage of the scenic landscapes for outdoor sketching and painting. The islands' natural beauty provides an inspiring backdrop for artistic endeavors.

- **Cultural Immersion:** Consider joining workshops incorporating elements of Scilly's cultural heritage. From traditional crafts to contemporary expressions, these experiences deepen your connection to the islands' creative spirit.

The Isles of Scilly's diverse landscapes and welcoming ambiance invite visitors to tailor their experiences to special interests. Scilly provides a canvas for personalized exploration, whether you find solace in birdwatching, seek to capture the islands' essence through photography or yearn to express your creativity in art and craft workshops. As you immerse yourself in your chosen passion, the archipelago unfolds as a realm of wonder, where each moment is an opportunity to connect with nature, culture, and the artistic spirit of these captivating isles.

Community and Sustainability

The Isles of Scilly, a sanctuary of natural beauty and cultural heritage, embodies a commitment to community and sustainability. As visitors explore this archipelago, they become integral participants in preserving the delicate ecosystems, supporting local traditions, and fostering a sustainable future. In this section, we delve into responsible travel practices and how supporting local businesses contributes to the community's well-being and the preservation of Scilly's pristine environment.

Responsible Travel Practices: Treading Lightly on Isles of Wonder

The Isles of Scilly, with their unique biodiversity and ecological significance, call for responsible travel practices that ensure the preservation of this paradise for generations to come. Embracing sustainable tourism is not just a choice; it is a shared responsibility to protect the natural wonders and cultural richness that define the islands.

Key Responsible Travel Practices:

1. **Stay on Designated Paths:** Respect the delicate ecosystems by staying on designated paths, especially in nature reserves and areas with sensitive flora and fauna. Follow any environmental guidelines provided by local authorities.

2. **Waste Reduction:** Minimize single-use plastics and disposables. Carry a reusable water bottle, use eco-friendly bags, and dispose of waste in designated bins. Participate in beach clean-ups if available.

3. **Wildlife Observation Etiquette:** When observing wildlife, maintain a respectful distance and avoid disturbing their natural behavior. Follow ethical guidelines for birdwatching, seal-watching, and other wildlife encounters.

4. **Energy and Resource Conservation:** Conserve energy by turning off lights and appliances when not in use. Use water wisely and be mindful of resource consumption, considering the islands' limited resources.

5. **Support Conservation Initiatives:** Contribute to local conservation efforts by participating in organized conservation activities or supporting organizations dedicated to preserving the unique ecosystems of the Isles of Scilly.

6. **Responsible Boating:** If engaging in water activities, choose operators who adhere to responsible boating practices. Avoid disturbing marine life, follow designated routes, and be aware of any guidelines for protecting underwater environments.

7. **Weather-Appropriate Gear:** Be prepared for variable weather conditions by packing weather-appropriate gear. This ensures your comfort and safety while reducing the need to purchase disposable items.

Local Conservation Initiatives:

1. **Isles of Scilly Wildlife Trust:** Support the Isles of Scilly Wildlife Trust, an organization dedicated to conserving the

islands' natural habitats and wildlife. Participate in guided walks and events organized by the trust to learn about and contribute to local conservation efforts.

2. **Seabird Recovery Project:** Contribute to the Seabird Recovery Project, a collaborative initiative to protect and restore seabird populations on the islands. Donations and participation in related activities help fund vital conservation work.

3. **Beach Clean-Ups:** Join organized beach clean-ups to actively contribute to maintaining the cleanliness of the shores. These community-led efforts help combat marine litter and protect the marine environment.

Supporting Local Businesses: Nurturing the Heart of Scillonian Culture

The vibrant community on the Isles of Scilly thrives through the support of locals and visitors alike. By choosing to patronize local businesses, travelers become vital contributors to the islands' economic sustainability and cultural preservation. From traditional markets to artisanal boutiques, each transaction fosters a connection to the community and ensures the continuation of Scilly's unique way of life.

Ways to Support Local Businesses:

1. **Local Markets and Shops:** Explore the bustling markets and shops at St. Mary's, offering a diverse array of locally produced goods. From handmade crafts to fresh produce, these businesses showcase the talent and craftsmanship of the local community.

2. **Art Galleries and Studios:** Visit art galleries and studios showcasing the work of Scillonian artists. Purchasing local art adds a unique piece to your collection and supports the thriving artistic community on the islands.

3. **Farmers' Markets:** Attend farmers' markets to sample and purchase fresh, locally sourced produce. Supporting local farmers not only ensures the freshness of your meals but also contributes to sustainable agriculture practices.

4. **Traditional Pubs and Restaurants:** Opt for traditional pubs and locally owned restaurants celebrating Scilly's culinary heritage. Many establishments use locally sourced ingredients, providing an authentic taste of the islands.

5. **Accommodations with Local Character:** Choose accommodations with local character, such as family-run bed and breakfasts or guesthouses. These establishments often offer a more personalized experience and contribute directly to the local economy.

6. **Participate in Local Events:** Attend local events, festivals, and community gatherings. Your participation enriches your cultural experience and supports the organizations and individuals who organize these events.

Community Initiatives:

1. **Local Arts and Crafts Workshops:** Join arts and crafts workshops by local artisans. These experiences provide an opportunity to learn new skills and contribute directly to the livelihoods of artists and craftspeople.

2. **Community Festivals:** Participate in community festivals that celebrate the cultural heritage of the Isles of Scilly. These events often involve local businesses, artists, and performers, fostering a sense of community pride.

3. **Heritage Preservation Projects:** Contribute to heritage preservation projects that aim to safeguard the architectural and historical treasures of the islands. Donations and support for initiatives that restore and maintain cultural landmarks play a crucial role.

As visitors traverse the Isles of Scilly, they become custodians of its natural and cultural treasures. The collective commitment to responsible travel practices and supporting local businesses ensures preserving the island's unparalleled beauty and the flourishing of its vibrant community. By treading lightly, respecting local traditions, and nurturing the economic vitality of the archipelago, travelers contribute to the ongoing legacy of the Isles of Scilly as a sustainable and thriving paradise.

Conclusion

In the embrace of the Atlantic's azure waters lies a hidden gem—the Isles of Scilly. This archipelago, a tapestry of natural wonders and cultural richness, invites travelers on a journey of exploration, connection, and preservation.

The Isles of Scilly unfold as a symphony of nature's beauty, where diverse ecosystems and pristine landscapes converge. Responsible travel practices become our guide, urging us to tread lightly on designated paths, minimize our environmental impact, and support local conservation initiatives. In doing so, we become custodians of the islands' delicate balance, ensuring that future generations can revel in the beauty that Scilly generously shares.

Woven into the Isles of Scilly fabric is a rich cultural tapestry shaped by centuries of history and maritime traditions. Ancient burial chambers, historic lighthouses, and charming villages offer glimpses into the lives of the Scillonian people. As visitors, our role extends beyond observation—we become participants in preserving and celebrating this cultural legacy.

Navigating the Isles of Scilly is an adventure in itself, where each mode of transportation contributes to the unfolding narrative. Aboard the Scillonian III ferry, soaring through the skies on the Skybus, or island-hopping on local boats, every movement is an opportunity to connect with the island's diverse landscapes and unhurried pace. Integration of these modes allows for a seamless exploration, each experience blending into the next like the gentle waves caressing the Scillonian shores.

The Isles of Scilly cater to various interests, inviting visitors to tailor their experiences. For birdwatching enthusiasts, the archipelago is a sanctuary where seabirds, waders, and migratory species dance in the sky. Photography aficionados find inspiration in the play of light on golden beaches, rugged cliffs, and historic landmarks. Art and craft workshops, nestled in the heart of the community, provide a canvas for creative expression, drawing on the islands' natural beauty as a muse.

As travelers, we are not mere observers but active participants in the sustainability and prosperity of the Isles of Scilly. Responsible travel practices ensure that our footprint is light, leaving the islands as pristine as we found them. By supporting local businesses—be they traditional pubs, artisanal boutiques, or family-run accommodations—we contribute to the community's economic vitality. The islands come alive through their landscapes and the stories of the people who call them home.

The Isles of Scilly, with their timeless allure, are a testament to the delicate balance between nature and community. Our journey through these isles reminds us that our connection to the environment and the communities we encounter is reciprocal. As stewards of this paradise, we must preserve its wonders for future generations. Our shared commitment to sustainability, responsible tourism, and local engagement ensures that the Isles of Scilly remain a beacon of inspiration, inviting travelers to write their chapters in the ongoing story of this Atlantic haven.

In bidding farewell to the Isles of Scilly, let us carry with us memories of landscapes and seascapes and a profound appreciation for the intricate web of life that thrives on these islands. May the echoes of seabirds, the rustle of windswept heathlands, and the warmth of Scillonian hospitality linger in our hearts, inspiring us to be mindful travelers, conscientious stewards, and lifelong advocates for the preservation of our planet's natural and cultural treasures. Until the next tide brings us back to these Isles of Wonder, may the spirit of Scilly accompany us on our continued journeys.

Printed in Great Britain
by Amazon

39025699R00056